LEGAL SOLUTION
DESIGN GUIDE

How to Design and Develop A Valuable
Legal Solution With Human Intelligence

DEBORAH VELLA

Thank you

Thank you for reading this book. It shows that you have a genuine interest in legal design and human intelligence, and the motivation to transform your skills to become a modern lawyer.

I used to be a traditional lawyer. It was a range of experiences over my career that helped develop my passion for building a law practice where I could use the power of human intelligence to help legal professionals. Those experiences taught me that being able to lead the development and delivery of your legal solutions to your clients is invaluable.

By developing my legal solutions, I've been able to create a business where I have a meaningful connection with my clients and followers every day. I'm also able to work efficiently, effectively and remotely, which means that I have the time and energy to enjoy life with my family. I love being a lawyer now!

I'd like you also to rediscover your passion for being a great lawyer, starting with challenging traditional ways of practice as you read through this guide. There is an immense sense of achievement which comes from designing and developing your first legal solution, no matter how small.

You will be one of the few innovative lawyers who lead the legal industry into modern practice, transforming the way we provide legal services for the better. You can redefine what it means to be a lawyer, and what that means for work and life balance. For this, I thank you.

I look forward to seeing the valuable legal solution that you design and develop and what you achieve for your clients. Please connect with us on social media so our community of like-minded legal professionals can also learn from you.

Facebook – https://www.facebook.com/supportlegal/

Linked In – https://www.linkedin.com/in/support-legal-online-documents-services/

Instagram - https://www.instagram.com/supportlegalau/

Twitter - https://twitter.com/AUsupportlegal

Thank you

Deborah

Contents

Do You Work Efficiently and Effectively?

Working efficiently and effectively means that you can work more productively at a higher level because you'll be spending far less time doing routine tasks.

You can manage those everyday tasks much better through a planned process. You can also spend more time doing what is important to you and more consistently identify opportunities for growth.

Do you know how you spend your time each week?

Can you meet your goals each week?

Are you surprised?

You need to think strategically about the processes for your work so that those processes work efficiently and effectively for you. You also need to make sure that your involvement in each of those processes should be a valuable use of your time. Otherwise, all you'll do is be busy.

That is why you need to design and develop valuable legal solutions to replace the legal services you currently provide.

Why do we provide legal services without a planned process?

"I don't know how to work any other way."

"I don't have the time to design legal solutions."

"I need to focus on doing the work that I can send invoices for now."

"I'm not sure my services are good enough to develop into a solution."

So many excuses!

The traditional way of providing legal services does not make much business sense anymore. And it is certainly not an efficient and effective way to work.

Enough with the excuses.

You cannot afford not to design and develop valuable legal solutions for your practice.

Do what you need to do to get it done.

- Deborah Vella

Can you design and develop legal solutions for your practice?

Imagine:

- You can confidently deliver your legal solution in difficult times.
- You are doing more of the work you love with the clients you admire.
- Being in control of how you spend your time working on matters, so you do not have to be busy or stressed.
- You have the time to work with your clients on a more strategic level or more matters for a higher income.
- You are looking forward to business development projects.

First, you must decide if you are ready to give it a go.

The ideas in this guide are for you if you:

- Can find at least 4 hours per week (in two-hour blocks),
- Would like to stop being so busy all the time,
- Are willing to start changing the way you work for the better, and
- Will commit to following through with implementing your legal solution.

Our ideas are not done-for-you solutions. If you are not ready to give it a go, then you won't see any benefits.

Are you ready?

Before You Start - Sort Out Your Time

Did you know? Our brains can work most productively if we keep to a routine. Make the most of this by dedicating at least 4 hours per week to your legal solution, preferably in two-hour blocks at the same times each week. Make sure each block is at a time when you'll be productive and won't be overwhelmed with "urgent" work to do instead.

Don't make excuses! Do what you need to do to make it happen.

You can use this time first to develop your legal solution and then deliver it. The key is to make sure you work productively. When you work on your legal solution at the same time each week, you'll soon notice that your brain is ready to work productively at that time. You'll also see that the people around you learn to leave you alone at these times too.

You could also keep a list of tasks handy that you can finish in less than 5 minutes each and work through the list whenever you have spare time between more extensive tasks. It's an easy way to energise your mind and feel great with some quick wins!

Let's start designing your solution!

1

Understand Legal Design and Human Intelligence

Legal design is all about looking at how we do what we do as lawyers and planning to do it more strategically. The key is designing how we do what we do to be human-centric. Human intelligence is applying concepts from psychology to legal design to make our work naturally more appealing to our clients. It is essentially recognising what we do subconsciously as experienced lawyers and using legal design to apply it to our legal solutions.

We need to take what we do as lawyers and use design thinking to turn our legal services into products and solutions. Legal products are a form of content that contains legal information but no legal advice. An example of a legal product is a document or a guide. Legal solutions are a combination of legal services which includes legal advice and legal products which solves a client's problem.

By designing legal solutions, we can focus on our clients and how the law applies to them.

There is a generally accepted process designing a good solution. The process is:

1. Gather information to understand the problem.
2. Define the users of the solution and how the problem will be solved.
3. Brainstorm different ideas.
4. Create a solution.
5. Test the solution.
6. Deliver the solution and refine it over time.

Trust the legal design process because it works. You'll find that different designers will use various techniques within these steps, depending on their perspective and their experience in reaching the desired outcome.

In this guide, we will use a design process specifically for creating a valuable legal solution. We'll also use some specific techniques to apply human intelligence to your design to make it naturally more appealing to your clients.

Get it done

1. Think about three processes that have changed in your life over the years and why the new methods are better for you.

2

Understand Your Clients' Problems

You need to have direct open discussions with your clients.

Select 5 to 10 clients that you trust, because you'll appreciate the information they give you. Either invite them for a group discussion for at least an hour or individual chats for at least 15-minutes. You might find that some clients are happy with a group forum, and others would prefer the privacy of a personal discussion.

The purpose of these sessions is to gather information about your clients and their problems. Even though you'll be using this information in your business development, you still need to maintain your clients' privacy. When you make your notes during the discussions, make sure you don't include any personal details.

You'll need to gather information about the basic attributes of your clients. You'll also need to gather your clients' thoughts about the problems they faced, when they started facing these problems, why they had to deal with these problems and how they dealt with these problems.

How should the discussion flow? You should use these open questions to start conversations on different points, and then ask the questions that come to mind following your clients' answers. To lead a good discussion, focus on what your client is saying and use more open-ended questions to get more information on a topic. Clarify what your clients have told you by restating their answers and asking a closed question to check if that is correct. When a client has finished discussing a topic, they will let you know. Then you can start with an open question on another subject to start the discussion again.

Give a small thank you treat or gift for your client's efforts.

While you're gaining a deep understanding of your clients' problems, your clients will tell you the solution that you need to create.

Gather information from your team (if you have one)

Have the same open discussions that you had with your clients with your team (if you work with one). This time focus on your teams' thoughts about your clients' problems.

Don't forget a small thank you treat or gift for your team's efforts.

Explore the data

Use the precious data in your client files and your website.

The purpose of exploring the data is to gather more information about your clients and online users to help you with your practice development. Again, you still need to maintain your clients' privacy. When you make your notes, make sure you don't include any personal details.

You'll need to gather information about:

1. The basic attributes of your clients and online users.
2. The problems your clients dealt with and the issues that led to online users searching for information.
3. When and why your clients started facing these problems.
4. What patterns in online searching data might indicate that users are experiencing other issues when looking for specific information.
5. How your clients dealt with these problems, and what keywords are the most popular in online searches.

Go through your old client files and gather relevant information and write down your thoughts as you read through the information.

Next, look at the data from your practice's website. Look at the basic attributes of the users on your site using analytics software and see how much time they are spending on each page. What information do they seem to be reading?

Also, try exploring data from keyword search tools and statistical information reporting services such as the Australian Bureau of Statistics.

What can you see from the information? What can you tell from what you don't see?

Check your understanding

There are a few techniques that you can use to check your understanding of your clients' problems. It will help you to shape the information you've just gathered into a good summary of your clients' and their problems.

The techniques are:

1. Identify relevant factors and conditions – Think about your clients' problems in terms of the time and money cost and how much physical, mental and emotional effort your clients needed to deal with the problem.
2. Visualise the problem – By now you will have a few narratives in your mind for different types of clients which covers the factors that lead into the problem, what the problem is and what the solution is. Talk through those narratives with a colleague or friend.

3. Draw diagrams – Take the information and draw some diagrams to show what the problem looks like from different perspectives.

4. Learn about the context – If your clients come from a specific industry, learn more about the industry so you can confidently understand why your clients' problems are problems for them.

5. Review your original notes – How similar were your thoughts than to the ideas you have now? What have you learned?

6. Follow up with clients – Does the information you have gathered make sense to you? If not, go back to your clients and ask your questions.

Create a summary for each different type of client and each of the problems. Try covering who the client is, what the problem is, when they experience the problem, why they experience the problem and how they tend to deal with the problem. Also, include notes on what the relevant factors and conditions are for this target client and problem. For example, consider the time and money cost, the effort they need to deal with the problem and whether the problem the same as for a wider group of people.

Understanding your clients' problems makes them real to you.

Get it done

1. Write down your thoughts.
2. Hold discussion sessions with clients that you trust.
3. Hold discussion sessions with your team (if you have one).
4. Explore the data.
5. Check your understanding.
6. Summarise your results.

3

Commit to a Target Client You Can Help and a Problem You Can Solve

Go through your summaries and decide which target client your practice can help. Then decide which of their problems your practice can solve.

Do what you need to do to be comfortable with the decision-making process but give yourself a deadline to make a decision. If you need to ask more questions, do that. If you need to research more, do that too. Give yourself a few days to think about it. However, give yourself a deadline for when you will have decided to avoid procrastinating.

You'll achieve your goals faster when you commit to a niche because you'll concentrate your attention on where it needs to be.

Here are some techniques you can use to make the decision-making process more comfortable:

1. Consider what you'll gain and what you'll avoid for each option– This will help you make the decision faster and be happy to fix any issues as you go along.
2. Beware of focusing on stereotypes – You need to consider only the information in the summaries.
3. Take your time if you need to – It's okay to stop and rethink.

Get it done

1. Commit to a target client your practice can help and a problem your practice can solve.

4

Get to Know Your Tech

It's time to do some googling and scrolling. Look into the different software options that are available and check out the features and pricing options.

While you're researching different options, note down the purpose and outcome that each software solution provides.

Website

Your practice probably already has a website, but do you know all of the features of it? Discover what features are available, their purpose and what outcomes they could offer.

If your practice doesn't have a website yet, have a look at the different hosting options. There are plenty of hosting providers that also provide templates and an editor so you can build your website with some useful features. Or you can organise for a developer to build a website for your practice.

Video Hosting Platforms

These platforms are a fantastic way to upload your videos and create a link for sharing them. You can create a channel for your practice if you wish and include a playlist of videos for your clients to watch. You can then use the links to each video that the platform generates to share specific videos in other ways, such as in emails or within your automated document interviews.

> Remember, merely using technology won't make your legal solution wonderful. Only you can make your legal solution wonderful with a great design that includes human connection.

Graphic Design

Quality graphic design platforms take the complexity of designing graphics and makes it simple to create beautiful images to use on your website, in your marketing and throughout your legal solution. There will tend to be a range of templates that you can use with a variety of ready-to-use content and your branding. The purpose of graphic design software will be to enhance the quality of the content that you develop for your solution. The outcome is that you'll have high-quality images that are ready to use.

Marketing Platform

Powerful marketing platforms help you to automate your marketing using landing pages for your offers and email sequences to subscribers. You might choose to use these functions to entice potential clients to take up your offers for your solution and use the email campaign functions to connect with potential clients for future offers.

If your practice already has a website, you might already have an account to a marketing platform. If not, there are many quality platforms from which to choose.

The purpose of a great marketing platform is to automate your marketing and methodically manage your communications so you can grow your practice. The outcome is that you'll have potential clients who are ready to take up the offers for your solution.

Chatbot Software

Chatbots are becoming a popular way to gather small amounts of information from people as they use a short chat format that people are generally very comfortable using.

You can use chatbots in a variety of ways for your practice, depending on what you would like to achieve. You could use a chatbot as a lead magnet to offer a quiz or other useful information in exchange for a person signing up to your email list. You could also use chatbots to answer common questions or to direct a person for where they can gain further assistance for their particular enquiry.

One of the key benefits of chatbots is that you can use them on your website or Facebook Messenger, so they are available whenever your target client wants to use one. The other key benefit is that you can create a summary of the information that you gather to use when you first meet with your target client.

Will the tech work for you?

Video Conferencing

Convenient video conferencing platforms will allow you to hold meetings, share files and chat messages and host or attend webinars. You can easily set up a private meeting room that you can use for each of your meetings and set up several features to help you host meeting the way you'd like to. All you'll need is a basic webcam and headset (if your webcam doesn't have a microphone built-in) which don't cost much from any store which sells computer or office supplies.

The purpose of great video conferencing software is to bring the meeting process securely online. The outcome is that you will be able to meet with your clients online without the inefficiencies of meeting in person.

Information Collection Software

Great information collection software will allow you to send requests for information to your client, provide a guide on the information you need and show them how to provide it to you. Your client will then receive automatic reminders (so you don't have to follow them up). The information will be well organised and available to download anytime.

The purpose of this kind of software is to improve the quality of information you receive through a streamlined process. The outcome is that you will have the information available in an organised way without the overwhelm, stress and potential errors caused by endless emails back and forth.

Document Automation Software

Essential document automation software will significantly reduce the time and cost of producing legal documents. You should be able to create custom automations for a variety of different purposes.

The purpose of excellent document automation software is to transform how your practice produces documents. The outcome is that you'll have documents that are ready for you to use within minutes.

Practice Management Software

Quality practice management software will efficiently and effectively manage the day to day operations of your practice, wherever and whenever you choose to work.

The purpose of powerful practice management software is to take care of all the routine tasks so you can spend more time on more valuable tasks.

What processes can you automate?

Electronic Signing

Using electronic signatures significantly reduces the costs and delays associated with having to print, sign and post documents and then wait for another party to return them. If you're still using paper and pen for documents that don't have to be signed in person, why?

The purpose of electronic signing platforms is to automate the process of getting documents signed. The outcome is that you'll have a signed agreement faster without the hassle.

Productivity Tools

There are many productivity tools available which will help reduce the time it takes to perform routine tasks. For example, using a booking form means that your clients can make appointments with you online without going back and forth by phone or email. Another example is workflow management software which helps you keep your tasks and any information that you need for those tasks together in one place.

Bring it all together

Discover How It Works

Look through the information about the software and find out how it works.

What content do you need to create to start using it? What information do you need to put in at the start of the process for each piece of software? What is the result at the end of the process within each piece of software?

How much time and money does each option cost? How hard would it be for you, your team and your clients to use each option? Considering these factors will help you decide which software would be best to use within your solution.

Understand How It Connects

You can use middleware or workflow software to transfer data between the available APIs of two pieces of software to create an automated process. While many software options include established integrations, this middleware or workflow software will help you where there aren't the established integrations you need, as long as the software makes its information available to use.

Get it done

1. Research different software options.
2. Discover how the various software options work.
3. Understand how to connect different software using middleware or workflow software.

5

Organise Your Documents

Which legal documents will you need as part of your solution? Why? Review them to check if they will help you achieve the solution to your target clients' problem. If not, update them, so they do. Then make sure they are easily accessible.

What information will you need to give to your client as part of the solution? How do you currently present that information? Think about whether you could turn the information you usually provide about the process for a matter into a simple guide that the client could download at the start of the solution and use to help them. It's quite easy to create a beautiful looking guide using the Canva software, and you can also quickly turn a Word document with your practice's branding into a pdf document.

Work out what information you'll need to gather and how you'll gather it

What information do you need to produce each of your legal documents? Note it down.

If you and your team will produce the documents manually, how do you intend to gather the information? Will you gather what information you can from sources other than your client and then collect the rest of the information from your client? Will you gather the information you need from your client in a meeting, by requesting they provide the information by email or giving them a form to complete?

Prepare a checklist, precedent email or form, so you don't miss out on gathering the information you need. If you're planning to send a checklist to your clients, why not prepare the checklist with your branding as a pdf document using graphic design software such as Canva? However, making a clear checklist in Word would be just as effective.

Do you know what information you need so you don't waste time gathering it?

Consider how you and your team will prepare the documents

If you or your team will produce documents manually, will you have a guide to ensure there is consistency in the drafting between authors? Will your practice have a Style Guide to make sure all of your legal documents are branded and presented consistently? You don't need to dictate how to prepare every detail, but it would be useful to have at least some high-level guidance to make sure your documents are prepared and presented as you intend.

If the solution will use automated documents and they are set up for your clients to complete the interviews, will the finished document be sent directly to your client or will the document be withheld for you and your team to review it first? Take a look at the publishing settings for each of your automated documents.

If the solution will use automated documents, do you intend for you and your team to complete the interviews while in a meeting with your clients? Will, you or your team, need to make further changes to the document or will you organise for it to be completed (and signed if required) during the meeting?

Think about the process of preparing the documents and how you'd like that process to fit within your solution. If you are planning to prepare the documents for your solution now manually, take some time to learn more about the world of automated documents and what you need to do to develop quality automated documents. You can always incorporate your automated documents into your solution later on.

When you are clear about exactly how you'll solve a problem, you stop worrying about whether or not you can solve it.

Get it done

1. Choose and review your legal documents.
2. Present information in a useful way for your clients.
3. Prepare any checklists, precedent emails or forms to gather information.
4. Prepare any guides for authors of your documents.
5. Set the publishing settings for your automated documents.

6

Design Your Solution

Using all the notes you've put together so far will help you design your solution without missing any essential elements. You might find that some of your earlier notes don't seem as wonderful anymore. That's okay because it means that you're developing your skills as a modern lawyer. Simply go back to the relevant step and go back over it to make sure you're happy with your notes from that step.

Your Overall Business Strategy

Your business strategy starts with your marketing strategy, which will attract potential new clients to your solution. Your marketing strategy then connects to your valuable legal solution, which will cover from the point when a target client decides to take up your offer to the point when you solve your new client's problem. You can use a final step within your solution for gaining reliable feedback and testimonials that leads into your practice's business development strategy.

Create your design

The design of your legal solution will start with your target client accepting the offer that you present for your solution and finish after you've solved your client's problem.

Gather together all of the notes you prepared during previous modules to reference as you go through this module.

Add the steps

Start by adding every step in the process, from start to finish. Your legal solution should ideally include between 5 and 10 steps, so the process is apparent.

For each step, decide what the purpose of the step is and what the desired outcome will be. The purpose of the step should explain why the step is necessary. The desired outcome should explain what result the software or person responsible for the task needs to achieve for that step before moving on to the next step.

You might have a couple of steps that need to repeat as a group until you reach the desired outcome for the last step in that group. If so, clearly mark which steps you or your team may need to repeat. You might also have one or two optional steps that only apply in certain situations. If so, clearly mark these steps as optional.

Refer back to the notes you took when you were getting to know your tech. Think about whether you are happy that some tech could carry out one or more of the steps in your design.

Add the tasks for each step

Under each step, add the tasks that the software or person responsible for that task needs to complete to achieve the desired outcome for each step.

For each task, describe the primary method that will be used to complete that task and decide what the desired output will be. Also, include a backup method for if the primary method fails to achieve the desired output.

When you describe the primary method that will be used, be clear about whether the task will be automated or whether you or your team will complete the task manually. If someone performs the task manually, include the details of any software that you or your team will use.

Be clear when describing the desired output, so you know what information is available for you to use within later tasks. If you know that a later task will need certain information before the software or person responsible can complete it, make sure you include the collection of that information in an earlier task.

You and your team will use the backup method if the main method doesn't result in the desired output. Make sure the backup method differs enough from the main method that it won't fail if the main method fails.

Ideally, there should be no more than a few tasks per step. If you have too many tasks, you will lose the focus on achieving the desired outcome for the step. Consider consolidating those tasks that software or the person responsible can achieve together. Some tasks may be larger than others or take longer than others to complete, and that's okay. There may even be some tasks that will need to be completed over more than one session or repeated.

When you see your finished design, you'll realise that it's also your plan to unlock potential in your practice that is far greater than the valuable legal solution you develop.

Add an information bank

Add a point under each task called 'Information Bank'. Go through each task and detail what information you have gathered from the client throughout that task. If you will be using software to automate some of the tasks, try to include as much detail as possible.

You'll soon see how much information you have gathered from the client at each task within your solution.

Add the links that connect each task

Between each task, add details of what action will link the tasks together and whether it will be an automated or manual action performed by a specific person. Also include the information that you will need to put into the link and what information you need to get out of the link for it to work.

The input information should be part or all of the information that is available from either the desired output of the previous task or the information banks from the previous tasks. For example, if the task were to send an email, you would need to know what the email address is from either information gathered in the last task or information you hold for that client. If you need information that is not available, you'll need to change earlier tasks to collect that information.

The output information should be all of the information that is needed for the next task unless the software or person responsible for the next task can draw it from the information bank.

By this point in creating your design, you will start to see how well your solution is coming together. Don't forget to link the end of your design back into your business strategy for maintaining your relationship with your client.

Refine your design to balance efficiency and effectiveness

Your solution needs to be the balance of efficiency and effectiveness that you believe is right for your target clients and your practice.

Look at the tasks and how they link together with other tasks. Are the methods in the groups of tasks the right balance of efficiency and effectiveness? Think about whether a group of tasks can be automated using software or whether someone should only perform particular tasks manually.

There are no right or wrong answers. What you consider to be the right balance of efficiency and effectiveness will depend on your practice, your target client and the purpose of your solution.

Here are some points to consider when choosing which method is the right balance:

- A method may be efficient, but it is not useful if it doesn't reliably reach the desired output.
- A method may be effective, but it is not useful if it takes too much time or manual input to reach the desired output.
- Ideal methods are those which improve simplicity. That is, methods that take less time, cost less money, take less physical effort, require less thinking or have a combination of these factors. Ideal methods are also similar to the methods that your clients use for other businesses and are not outside what your clients would do in their normal daily life.

Incorporate all professional requirements that apply

Your solution needs to meet all the professional requirements that apply to your solution, such as the requirements relating to client engagement, trust accounting, and performing checks for the quality of the work.

As an experienced lawyer, you will already be aware of the professional requirements that relate to the areas of law that you have experience practising in. Now is an excellent opportunity to review those professional requirements and make sure that the design of your solution meets all of the requirements.

Also, if you consider that part of your solution is not within the definition of 'legal services' within professional regulations or in your practice's professional indemnity insurance policy, make sure you also have appropriate business insurance in place.

You should check the professional requirements and make your own decision as to what applies to your solution and how it applies. Add points to your solution to meet these requirements now.

Add a task to ask for feedback and testimonials consistently

By consistently asking for honest feedback from your clients, you will find out what parts of your solution work well and what parts need improvement. You should openly ask your clients to get the best results, so they have an opportunity to say what they think. One way to do this is by having a call with your client and asking open questions. Another approach might be to send them an email and ask them to complete some open-ended questions in a survey. You could also ask them to leave an online review for your practice (just send them the link to add one).

Make sure you also consistently ask for testimonials from your clients that gave your practice excellent feedback, together with their permission to use the testimonial as part of your marketing strategy. You don't necessarily need to disclose your client's name or details of their matter within the testimonial but having a collection of honest testimonials about the success of your solution will be very useful in your marketing strategy.

Get it done

1. Create your design using steps, tasks, an information bank and links.
2. Refine your design to balance efficiency and effectiveness.
3. Incorporate all the professional requirements that apply to your solution.
4. Add a task to ask for feedback and testimonials.

7

Apply Human Intelligence

Applying human intelligence means to apply concepts is applying concepts from psychology to legal design to make our work naturally more appealing to our clients. It is essentially recognising what we do subconsciously as experienced lawyers and using legal design to apply it to our legal solutions.

There are seven core concepts of human intelligence that you need to apply. They are:

1. Client involvement.
2. Personalisation.
3. Positive experience.
4. Understandability.
5. Ways to prevent mistakes.
6. Good flow.
7. Simplicity.

There is no right or wrong way to do this. You decide on the balance that will work for your solution. What you include and how you include it is entirely up to you.

You might like to focus on some concepts rather than others, and that is okay. However, the ideas will work more effectively if they are applied together with others.

Some of the software you choose to use will incorporate aspects of human intelligence as part of its design.

The software you use is only as useful as the content you create for it. So, make sure your content uses human intelligence.

1. Client involvement

Your solution should include some tasks that your clients can do themselves.

Why not create a checklist of information for your client to gather? Are there any small tasks that your client can do straight away for an easy win?

Can you design the interview of your automated document so your client can complete it themselves?

Perhaps you could prepare a guide for what will happen during your solution and ask them to read it? Why not create a Facebook group on a relevant topic and invite them to engage with you and others who are interested.

Go to your design and add in the tasks that you've chosen. Make sure you mention the tasks that your client will need to do at the start of your solution, so they are aware that they will be coming up.

2. Personalisation

Your solution should always be personalised to your client unless there is a specific reason not to. The main reason not to use personalisation is if the content would not create a positive experience for your client.

Go through your design and consider all the points when you communicate with your client. For example, when you send an email, when there is a meeting or when you invite them to read information.

You can personalise this content automatically by using fields that you gather. For example, if you are sending an email through email marketing software, including a field for the person's first name. You would have collected this information when they signed up. In the design of your automated documents, you can use their name and any answers they provide in the interview within later questions in the interview.

If you or your team will be completing the task manually, make sure you already have the information you need to create a personalised experience. For example, know your client's name and all the information they have already provided and make sure you have the information available during your meeting. Ahead of time, think about what parts of your meeting are relevant to this client and stick to that!

When you invite a client to read information, think about whether it is appropriate to personalise that information. If the information is negative, it might be best to use personalisation in the email, inviting them to read an attached document but keep the content of the attachment objective. If the information is positive, see whether you can personalise some of the information to explain what it means for them.

Human intelligence is the key to designing solutions which are naturally appealing to clients.

Without it, even the most technologically advanced solutions will always be limited by their artificial constructs.

- Deborah Vella

3. Positive experience

Your solution should create a positive experience for your client.

Go through your design and make sure that any content that your client sees uses plain, positive language that focuses on them. For example, all emails, information that you present to them and the interview in your automated documents.

Now go through your design and identify the tasks that your clients will do. Make sure that you explain what to do in the task, how to do it and what defines a successful outcome. Then make sure that you provide all of the information that they need to succeed with the task.

Finally, include points within your design where you reflect and celebrate the little wins that you and your client achieve throughout the solution. Congratulate your client in a quick email or specifically mention the success next time you meet.

4. Understandability

Your solution should provide enough information to your client, so they always understand what to expect, what you and your team are doing for them and what they need to do.

Go to the start of your design. Include a summary of your solution, so your clients know what to expect during your solution. Try not to bombard your client with only text. Consider creating a short video for your clients to watch, which introduces your practice and explains what will happen during the solution.

Now, review the points you communicate with your clients, such as with emails, phone calls or meetings. Make sure you include information about what you and your team are doing, what they need to do (even if it's just to wait for you) and what they should expect to happen next. Including useful information can be as easy as opening your emails with one line about what is happening and finishing them with one line for what will happen next. For automated processes, include this in the content now. For manual processes, include an obvious reminder that will help you get into the habit of doing this every time (such as a note near your computer screen).

Finally, go through your design for all the points at which your client would need to make a decision. Include information to explain the available options, how to choose the best option and how to communicate that selection. Think about whether you can include a short guide that includes a good balance of images and text. Again, if you'll do this process manually, make sure there are points before your task where you prepare this information so you can tell your client.

5. Ways to prevent mistakes

Your solution should minimise the chance of your client making a mistake.

Look through your design and consider when your client could make a mistake. What are the most likely mistakes? Why?

Now include ways to prevent those mistakes from happening. Do this by adding warnings for your client that if a particular situation applies, they should stop and contact you for assistance. When asking your client to perform a task or make a decision, make sure that they have enough information (that is relevant to them) to understand what they need to do, how they need to do it and how to communicate their answer to you. And if you need to present options to your clients to choose from, make sure you only show options that are relevant and in a way that is meaningful to them.

6. Good flow

Your solution should flow well from start to finish with minimal interruptions or changes.

Consider the methods that you are asking your clients to use to perform tasks. Are they comfortable using those methods? Are the methods the same methods that they use to communicate with other service providers? If your clients love email, use it. If your clients prefer using an app on their phone to receive reminders, use it.

Look over your design and see how many interruptions there are which might have a "stop-start" effect? Can each person successfully finish the task that they are assigned to do, or do they have to do part of the task and then wait for something else to happen? It is far better to give a client a smaller task that they will complete successfully, then give them another small task later than give one enormous task that seems like it will never end. Aim for smaller tasks with easy wins to build confidence. Avoid larger tasks that clients have to worry about remembering to complete. In this fast-paced world, your tasks will not be the only ones competing for your clients' attention.

Finally, consider how many changes there are for your client and your team as they work through your solution. There might be changes between methods for different tasks or starting one task, then changing back to another. See what you can do to minimise the number of changes by grouping similar tasks together. Finally, make sure that the methods you use in your design are reliable, so you only need to use the backup method in exceptional circumstances.

Do not underestimate the power of simplicity.

It can take a lot of effort to remove everything that is not necessary for your solution, so you have a solution that is simple, effective and efficient.

– Deborah Vella

7. Simplicity

For your client, your solution should be as simple as possible.

Look at your design from the perspective of your client. What happens, and when? What do they need to do? Do you think you could refine the design to make the process simpler for your clients?

Look at the little things and use common sense. Can you reduce the time and money that someone will need to spend to perform a task if you use another method? For example, try to hold a video conference that a client can access using their smartphone in any location rather than requesting an in-person meeting which comes with travel and maybe someone to care for family members.

Try reducing the physical, mental and emotional effort they need to use by making the methods you use similar to something clients are already comfortable doing. For example, it might be easier for a client to take a photo of something and email it to you from their phone rather than asking them to make a photocopy and post it to you.

Finally, think about whether any part of the process might be out of the ordinary for your clients and add something that will help them feel comfortable. For example, if you are sending a document for electronic signature, briefly explain they need to follow the prompts in the software.

Aim to remove everything that is not necessary for your solution, so you have a solution that is simple, effective and efficient.

Check that your design makes sense and meets your goals

This step is the final stage of refining your design.

Go through each possibility of your design from start to finish and make sure it makes sense. Make sure you look at the journey for your clients, and the journey for you and your team.

Read through each possibility out loud like you would read a story and test the story out on your team, family or friends. Think about the original goals for your solution and make sure your design will meet those goals.

If you find that you've missed something or think that a change would be better, refine your design until you are happy that it works.

Get it done

1. Incorporated the core concepts behind human intelligence into the design of your solution.
2. Check that your design makes sense.

8

Develop Your Solution

You have everything you need to build your solution. It's time to put it all together!

Create great content

Your target clients want to read, hear and watch content that comes from you and your team. It has never been easier to create an image, take a photo, record a short video, or write clear text for throughout your solution. Do it!

Go through your design and list out the content that you need to prepare in two sections. In the first section, add the content that your solution will present to your client. In the second section, add the content that you and your team will use yourselves (such as checklists or templates). Include notes for what each piece of content needs to contain according to your design.

Now focus on creating that content. All of the content in the first section of your list should focus on your client. All of the content in the second section of your list should focus on you and your team. Once you have all of your content prepared, putting together your solution will be easier.

Develop your solution

Work through one step at a time to develop your solution. Then you'll be able to focus on getting each step working before you move onto the next.

If you aren't comfortable using certain features of the software, use the features that you are comfortable with to deliver the outcome that you need. Over time, you can learn more about those features and then refine your solution.

You might even prefer to work with experienced professionals on your team to develop part or all of your solution. Experienced professionals will be able to help you achieve what you intend because they know exactly how to do it.

If you don't have much money to spend, don't worry! Your solution doesn't need to be as magnificent as a high budget movie! What is important is that it provides a solution to your client's problem. Over time, you can gain assistance from other professionals to develop it further.

Focus on content that comes from you.

Set a price based on the value of your solution

The value of your solution has nothing to do with the costs of developing and delivering the solution. Essentially, the value of your solution to your target client is how much they are willing to pay for the benefit that your solution offers. The value will be higher if your target clients believe that your solution will be able to solve their problem with minimal demands on their time, money and physical, mental and emotional efforts. If you've added human intelligence to your solution, these demands will already be at a minimum.

Look back at everything that you are offering your target client and list what your solution means for them. What benefits will your clients gain? What problems will they avoid? What is the value of the time, money, physical, mental and emotional efforts that your target clients will save because of your solution? What will your client gain by establishing an ongoing working relationship with your practice? Read over your notes and see just how much value you are providing. Remember, you and your team will be delivering the solution with your unique style.

Now, select a price that you believe reflects the value of your solution. Come up with one price for the solution. One price will make it much easier for your marketing.

If you'd like to, consider adjusting the products and services you include in your solution so you can create a version of your solution for different levels of your target client's needs. For example, you might be able to offer a version of your solution that your clients can mostly follow themselves, a version that you work together on and a version that involves additional investments of your time. Your target clients will generally choose the option that they prefer.

Test out your pricing against your practice's needs. What are the time and money costs of developing, maintaining and delivering your solution? How many solutions (of each variation) do you need to sell to maintain a certain income? Are you able to commit the time to help make that happen?

Your pricing doesn't need to be perfect straight away, as you can refine your solution and adjust its price over time. Other factors can impact the value of your solution over time, such as the target clients' belief that your solution is in high demand and that you and your team can be trusted.

Stay away from working out a price based on estimated billable hours because the time you spend performing tasks does not correlate with the value that your solution provides to your client. Also, avoid making things cheap or trying to compete with others on price. You are unique, and only your practice can provide your solution to your clients. Don't compare yourself to others!

Get it done

1. Create the content that your solution needs.
2. Develop your solution.
3. Set a price for your solution that reflects its value to your target client.

9

Test Everything

The aim of testing everything is for you to know that your solution works and trust that it is reliable.

Try everything several times. Then try it one more time.

Test it across all devices to make sure all of the steps work how you intend for them to work.

Ask your team (or your friends) to try out your solution as if they were a client and practice delivering all of the steps.

If you don't feel comfortable with the way a step works, look at the tasks within that step to see what is happening. Is a link missing? Is a person that is responsible for a task not able to complete the task? Is there another reason why it isn't working?

Go back and refine the tasks until they work together to reach the outcome that you need to be able to move on to the next step in the solution.

If you find yourself worrying that a step may not work properly, test it again and again until you are comfortable that it does work reliably. If you find yourself constantly changing things to try to make them "perfect", stop.

You will find mistakes during this testing process, and that is okay. That's why you are testing everything. When you find a mistake, fix it and test it again. Then move on.

When you trust that your solution works reliably, you will have far more confidence when you deliver it to your clients.

Get it done

1. Test every aspect of your solution.
2. Refine your solution (but only if you need to).

10

Deliver Your Solution

Join your marketing strategy to the first step in your legal solution. The connection should be the point at which a target client chooses to take up your offer and engage your practice to provide your solution.

What that connection looks like will depend on your marketing strategy. If you are using an online marketing strategy, you might have a landing page where the target client accepts your offer. Or you might simply receive a phone call or email from a target client who is ready to take up your offer.

You and your team can now solve your target client's problem efficiently and effectively, simply by following your well-designed legal solution.

Be proud of what you and your team have achieved! Your new clients will pick up on your confidence and enjoy engaging with you even more.

Your design includes checks for you and your team to make sure your legal solution is working well. Keep up with those checks as a way to maintain the integrity of your solution. If there is a problem, don't worry. Fix it, test it and move on.

Watch how you and your legal team perform with your new legal solution. See if you notice any patterns which might turn into ideas for further developing your range of legal solutions.

Thank clients for their feedback and use the testimonials they provide. Most importantly, celebrate all of the little wins!

To successfully deliver your new legal solution, you need to integrate your solution within your practice and stop any temptation to revert to traditional ways of providing legal services to your new clients.

If you feel like you're not promoting or delivering the solution to the best of your ability, think about your motivations for delivering the solution. Think about the reasons that initially motivated you to take this course. Why did you want to design and develop the legal solution that you created? What will delivering this legal solution mean to you and your team?

Look at all of the skills you have learned during this course. Look at the incredible legal solution that you and your team have developed! Think about how you and your team will be able to help your clients on a higher level, simply by using the legal solution that you designed. Are you now more motivated to commit to delivering your legal solution well every time a target client takes you up on your offer?

If you still feel like you aren't able to commit to your legal solution completely, that's okay. Keep providing your other legal services as you always have for as long as you feel comfortable. Use your legal solution to replace just one of your legal services. As you and your team deliver your legal solution more often, you will gain more motivation to provide it!

If you or your team are delivering your solution and something goes wrong, don't panic! Move to the backup task, fix the problem and move on. Know that you can always step in and take over any task that needs doing. When things go wrong unexpectedly, we can feel disappointed, frustrated or even as if we have failed. That's normal. We will reduce these feelings but quickly fixing the issue and trying again.

When you start to see the results of delivering your legal solution, celebrate them! Treat yourself and your team when you achieve your goals or have an unexpected win, no matter how small. Enjoy the benefits that your legal solution brings to your practice, and you and your team personally.

Enjoy the benefits!

Get it done

1. Connect your marketing strategy to your legal solution.
2. Start delivering your legal solution to your new clients.

11

Refine Your Solution Over Time

One of the most important processes in a successful business is the feedback and refining process. This process gives you honest feedback to make changes to improve your solution and your offer.

The direct feedback you receive from the clients and your team members who follow your legal solution is pure. Your feedback may be overwhelmingly positive, and at times, it may be negative. It is how you understand it and what you do with it that will have a powerful impact.

Setting up a simple system to gain honest feedback effortlessly and reliably is critical. If you haven't included in your solution yet, go back and design it in now.

Your feedback system should have three key elements. First, you should ask for feedback promptly. That's why an automated email sent immediately after the last task in the solution is ideal. Second, you should ask and allow for honest feedback. The idea is to prevent a situation where your client may not feel comfortable offering honest feedback. You can ask for honest feedback through an anonymous questionnaire with open-ended questions rather than asking the lawyer that they had been working with to ask your client about their experiences working with them. Third, you should ask the same questions of every client in every matter to get reliable results. That's why automating your feedback system is ideal.

If the specific feedback is positive, ask those clients for a testimonial for your practice. You'll need to do this by including a question in your questionnaire to ask the client if they would be willing to provide a testimonial that you can use for marketing purposes. So go back and add this question now. The client can either leave an anonymous testimonial in your feedback questionnaire or leave their name and contact details for someone from your practice to contact them directly to collect a testimonial.

Making sure you, your team and your practice evolve with modern times is critical.

If the specific feedback is neutral or negative, be thankful rather than angry. It means that your client has gone out of their way to provide honest feedback for you to use so you can improve your solution. If a client didn't want to help you, they wouldn't have bothered to answer the questionnaire at all. When you look over the feedback, consider:

1. Is the feedback similar to other clients or team members?
2. What does the feedback say directly and indirectly?
3. Does the feedback apply to a specific point or from a specific point in the solution?

4. Did the client mention why they provided the feedback that they did?

Now consider all of the feedback together. Can you see any patterns in the feedback? Are there any questions raised by gaps in the feedback? Is the feedback generally positive, neutral or negative?

How can you use the feedback given to you to refine your solution? If there is an apparent mistake, simply fix it and move on. If the feedback suggests that something else is going on, test your understanding of what the problem might be against your solution. Are there relevant factors and conditions in your solution which lead to the issue? What other clues do you have? See if you could visualise the problem or draw a diagram to understand when it occurs. Then consider what changes you could make to your solution to refine it.

You don't have to refine your solution every time you receive neutral or negative feedback. But it's a good idea to at least monitor any potential issues so that you can make adjustments if and when you think it's necessary.

By creating a reliable feedback system and regularly reviewing the feedback you receive, you will have an incredible opportunity to refine your solution continually. Over time, your solution will improve and even evolve to meet your target clients' changing needs.

You can also use this feedback regularly as part of your business development strategy. It is a wonderful source of information to generate ideas to encourage growth and profitability.

Your strength lies in your ability to gratefully listen to feedback and continually improve.

Get it done

1.   Create a reliable system for refining your legal
     solution, so it continually evolves.

How We Can Support You

Automated Document Design and Development Solutions

Our Automated Document Design and Development Solutions are for busy legal professionals to design and develop quality, highly customisable automated legal documents for their practice.

We have a range of done-for-you or work-with-you solutions to help you design and develop quality, highly customisable automated legal documents.

Learn To Design With Human Intelligence

We have a range of courses that teach you how to use legal design and apply human intelligence to your work.

You have the opportunity to learn valuable skills to become a modern lawyer.

Discover more at www.supportlegal.com.au.

Printed in Great Britain
by Amazon